LIFE
HACKS*

BY **ANNABEL STAFF**

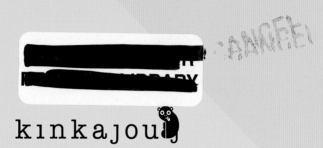

*LIFE HACKS
PUBLISHED BY **KINKAJOU**

A CATALOGUE RECORD FOR THIS BOOK IS AVAILABLE FROM THE BRITISH LIBRARY.

PHOTOGRAPHY BY **ANNABEL STAFF** ANNABELSTAFF.COM
DESIGN BY **NIC DAVIES** SMARTDESIGNSTUDIO.CO.UK

KINKAJOU IS AN IMPRINT OF FRANCES LINCOLN LIMITED
74-77 WHITE LION STREET, LONDON N1 9PF, UNITED KINGDOM.

ISBN: 978-0-7112-3758-2

PRINTED IN CHINA

9 8 7 6 5 4 3 2

TO VIVIENNE, FOR ALL THE LOVE,
SUPPORT AND MOTIVATION YOU GIVE
ME EVERY SINGLE DAY, YOU ARE LIKE
NO OTHER. I LOVE YOU.

LOOK I MADE A BOOK, HIGH FIVE!

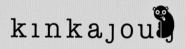

SPAGHETTI LIGHTER

LIGHT A STICK OF UNCOOKED SPAGHETTI FOR HARD TO REACH CANDLE WICKS

CORD SPRING

USE A SPRING FROM AN OLD PEN TO PREVENT YOUR CHARGER CABLES FROM BREAKING

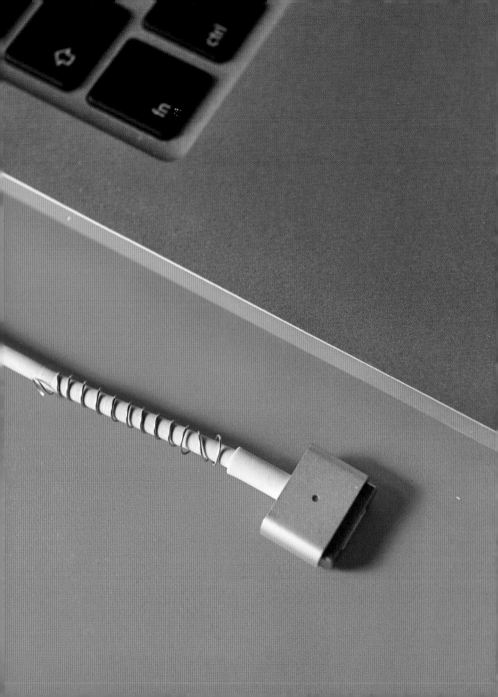

RED PEN BLACK INK

SWITCH THE INK FROM A BLACK PEN INTO A RED PEN - BECAUSE NO ONE STEALS RED PENS!

PERFECT ICE PACK

MAKE A REUSABLE AND FLEXIBLE ICE PACK BY MIXING ONE PART ALCOHOL TO TWO PARTS WATER IN A FREEZER BAG - RELEASE AS MUCH AIR AS POSSIBLE BEFORE FREEZING.

RUBBING ALCOHOL

70% Isopropyl Alcohol by volume

FOR EXTERNAL USE ONLY
• Serious gastric disorders will result if taken internally
• Keep away from Fire and Flame.
• Keep out of the reach of children.

Astringent
Rubbing Lotion

Net 500 mL

RED PEN YELLOW PAPER

YOU WILL REMEMBER SOMETHING BETTER BY WRITING IT DOWN WITH RED INK ON YELLOW PAPER

WINEGLASS DIP

USE A WINEGLASS AS A CONVENIENT DIP HOLDER

LEMON
CLEANER

REMOVE WATER
STAINS BY RUBBING
THEM WITH LEMON

VINEGAR CLEANER

TIE A BAG OF WHITE VINEGAR ONTO YOUR SHOWER HEAD AND LEAVE OVERNIGHT TO REMOVE BUILD-UP

BATTERY BOUNCE

DROP A BATTERY
VERTICALLY ONTO
A HARD SURFACE
- IF IT BOUNCES
MORE THAN ONCE
IT'S DEAD, IF IT
DOESN'T IT'S FRESH

PAINT
BAND

WRAP AN ELASTIC
BAND OVER A PAINT
CAN AND USE IT
TO WIPE YOUR
BRUSH TO KEEP
THE CAN CLEAN

VELCRO REMOTES

USE VELCRO
TO STORE YOUR
REMOTE CONTROLS
IN A CONVENIENT
PLACE SO YOU
DON'T LOSE THEM

ICE WATER

HALF FILL A BOTTLE WITH WATER; FREEZE HORIZONTALLY, THEN FILL THE REST WITH FRESH WATER FOR ICE WATER ON THE GO

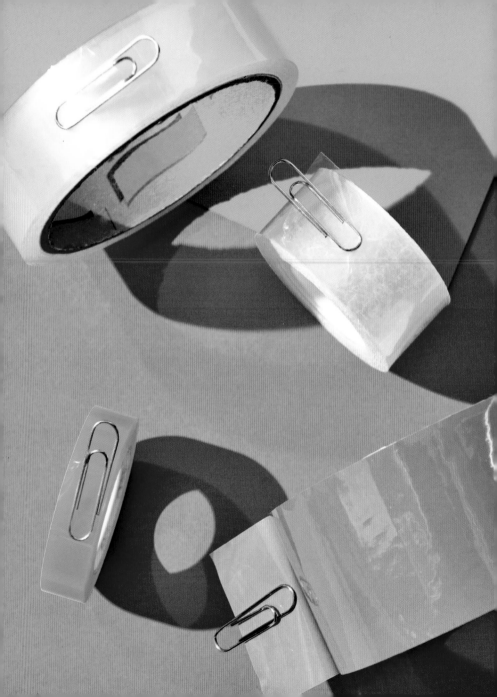

PAPERCLIP TAPE

STICK A PAPER CLIP TO STICKY TAPE SO YOU CAN ALWAYS FIND THE START

FROZEN GRAPES

FROZEN GRAPES COOL DOWN YOUR WINE WITHOUT WATERING IT DOWN

VARNISH KEYS

TELL YOUR KEYS APART BY PAINTING THEM WITH COLOURED NAIL VARNISH

CUPCAKE

SPLIT A CUPCAKE IN HALF AND INVERT THE TOP FOR MESS FREE EATING

PEG NAIL

USE A CLOTHES
PEG TO HOLD NAILS
WHILE YOU HAMMER
TO AVOID HITTING
YOUR FINGERS

SQUEEGEE

USE A SQUEEGEE TO
LIFT HAIR AND LINT
FROM CARPETS AND
FURNISHINGS

BOBBLES

DEPIL CLOTHING BY LIGHTLY RUNNING A RAZOR OVER IT

VARNISH BUTTONS

PAINT CLEAR NAIL VARNISH ON BUTTONS TO STOP THEM FALLING OFF

BANANA

OPEN A BANANA
FROM THE BOTTOM
TO AVOID BRUISING

- IT'S HOW MONKEYS DO IT!

FOLDBACK CLIPS

ATTACH FOLDBACK CLIPS TO YOUR DESK TO ORGANISE YOUR CABLES

ICE LOLLY

USE A CUPCAKE WRAPPER TO CATCH DRIPS

EGG BOTTLE

SQUEEZE A PLASTIC
BOTTLE OVER EGG
YOLK TO SEPERATE
IT FROM THE WHITE

CAN OPENER

USE A CAN OPENER TO OPEN STUBBORN PLASTIC PACKAGING

BUTTER

HEAT A GLASS WITH HOT WATER, EMPTY, AND PLACE OVER BUTTER TO SOFTEN QUICKLY WITHOUT MELTING

JEWELLERY

TALCUM POWDER
MAKES JEWELLERY
EASIER TO UNTANGLE

#28

KEYBOARD STICKY NOTE

USE THE GLUED END OF A STICKY NOTE TO LIFT LINT FROM YOUR KEYBOARD

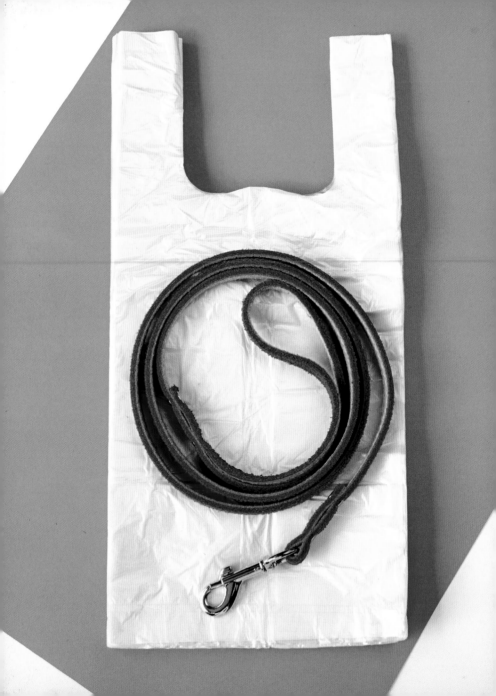

29

NAPPY
SACK

NAPPY SACKS
MAKE A CHEAPER
AND FRESHER
ALTERNATIVE TO
DOG POOP BAGS

30

ZIPPER RING

USE A KEYRING TO KEEP YOUR FLIES FROM COMING UNDONE